ME AND MY

Copyright 2024 © Darey and Karen Jolley

Printed in the United States of America. All rights reserved. No portion of this book may be reproduced, stored in a retrieval system, or transmitted in any form or by any means-electronic, mechanical, photocopy, recording, scanning, or other-except for brief quotations in critical reviews or articles, without the prior written permission of the publisher. Unless otherwise identified, Scripture quotations are taken from the New International Version, copyright © NIV®. Copyright © 1973, 1978, 1984 by International Bible Society. All rights reserved.

Published by ATTN Publishing 4020 Freedom Drive
Charlotte, NC 28208
Printed in the USA
ISBN 979-8-9889665-3-1

A long time ago a little boy named Darey lived on a farm with lots of animals.

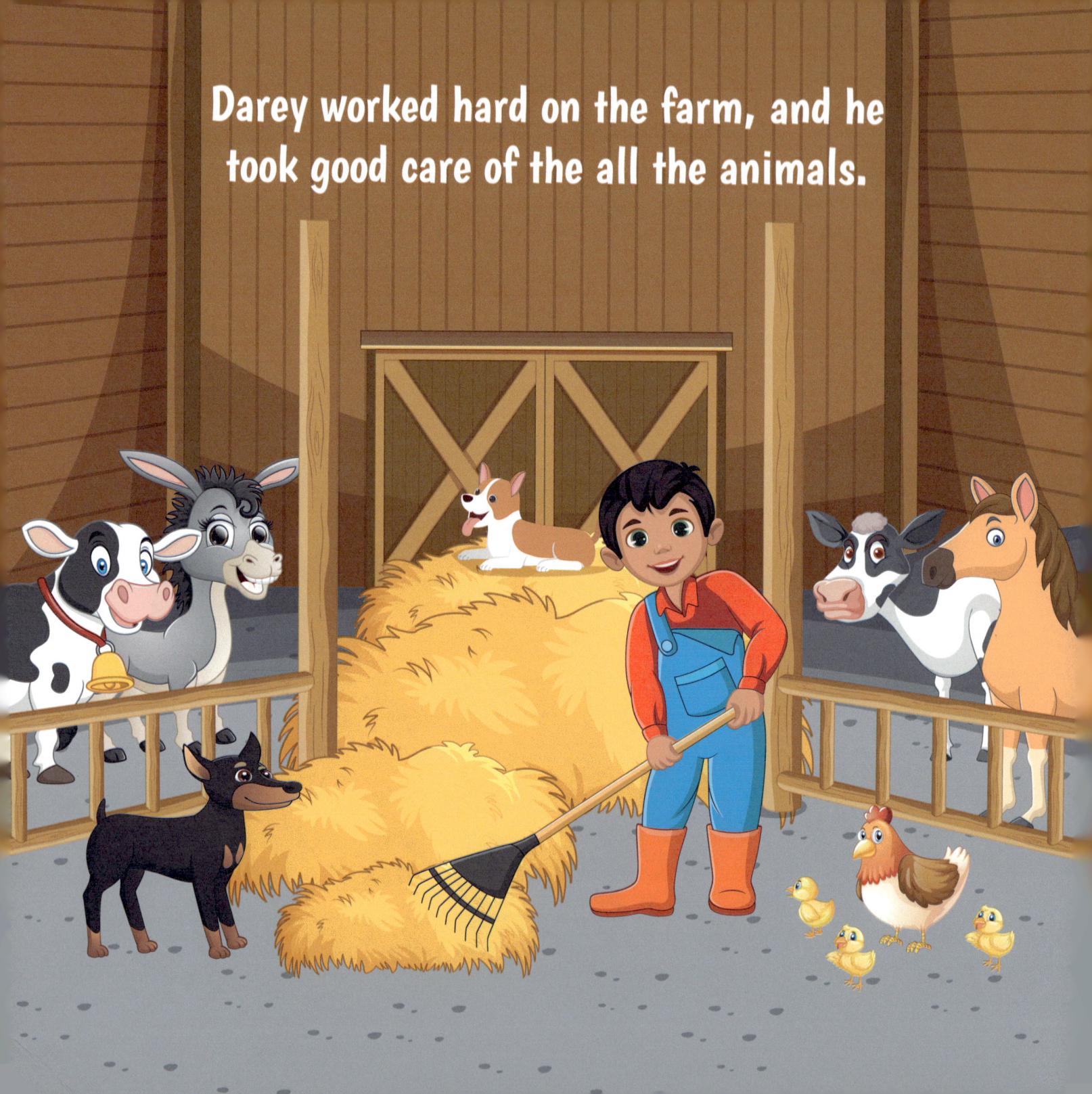
Darey worked hard on the farm, and he took good care of the all the animals.

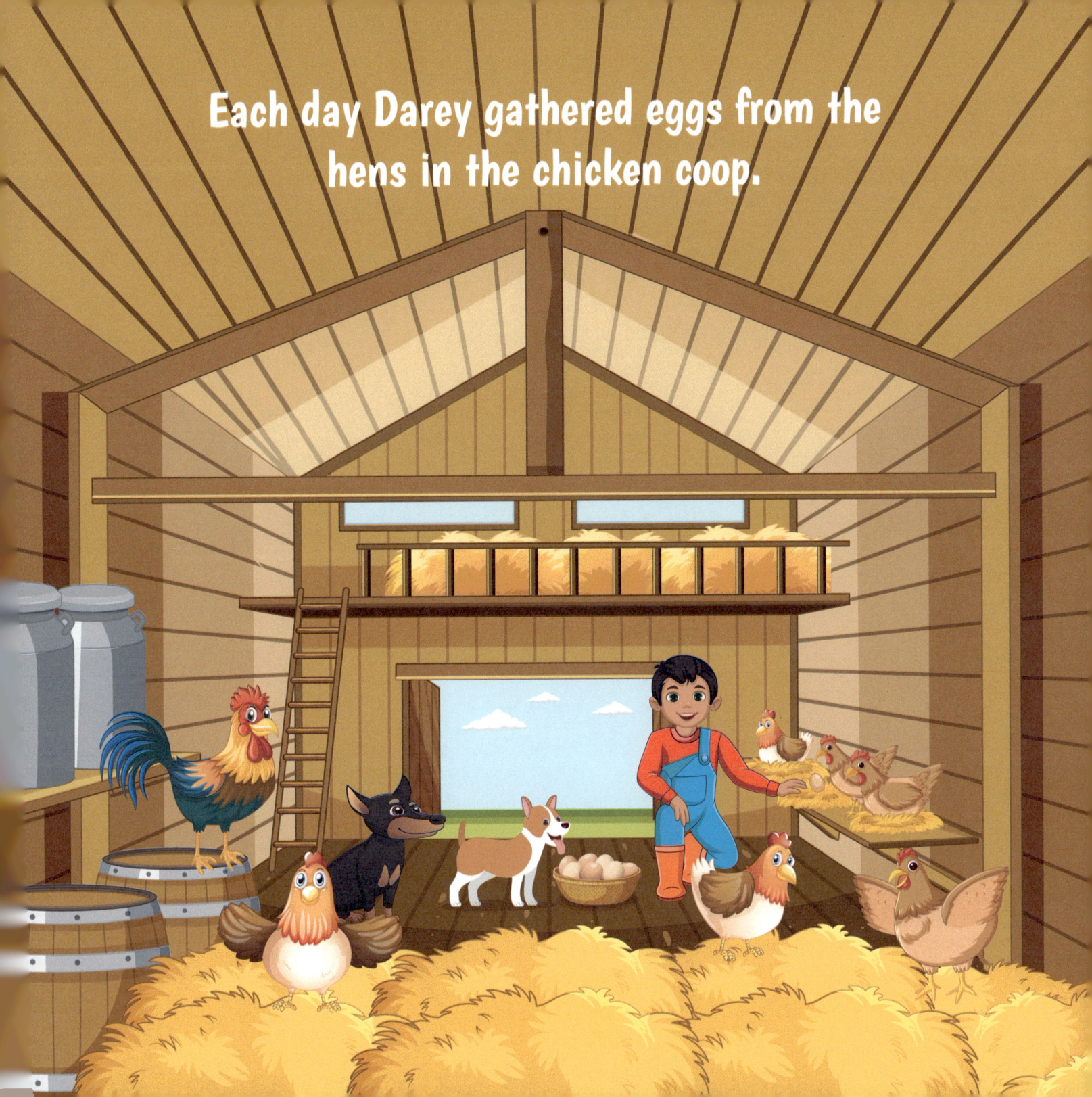

Yellow ducklings waddled behind him as he worked on the farm.

Mabel the cow provided warm milk for breakfast.

Tom the turkey strutted around with his proud chest puffed out.

The big pigs grunted and the baby pigs squealed when Darey brought them their breakfast.

In the garden, pink-nosed bunnies nibbled on the tops of carrots Darey had planted.

In the pasture, fluffy white sheep quietly grazed on grass while frisky young goats butted heads.

Each day Darey and his horse, Jerry, would go for a ride. Jerry loved to gallop!

Darey loved all the animals, even the stubborn donkey, Sam.

On Sundays, Darey got up early to feed all the animals, and then he went to church.

Darey loved to go to church, and one day he learned about a special Bible verse that talks about animals.

Proverbs 12:10 says that a righteous man takes care of his animals.

Darey asked the teacher, "What is a righteous man?" The teacher said, "A righteous person is someone who has asked Jesus to live in their heart."

Darey was excited to learn this because he had asked Jesus into his heart. He knew he was righteous!

Darey wanted to obey God's word. He remembered what Proverbs 12:10 said and he wanted to take good care of his animals.

Sometimes Darey would see people who weren't caring for their pets. Some people would even hurt their animals.

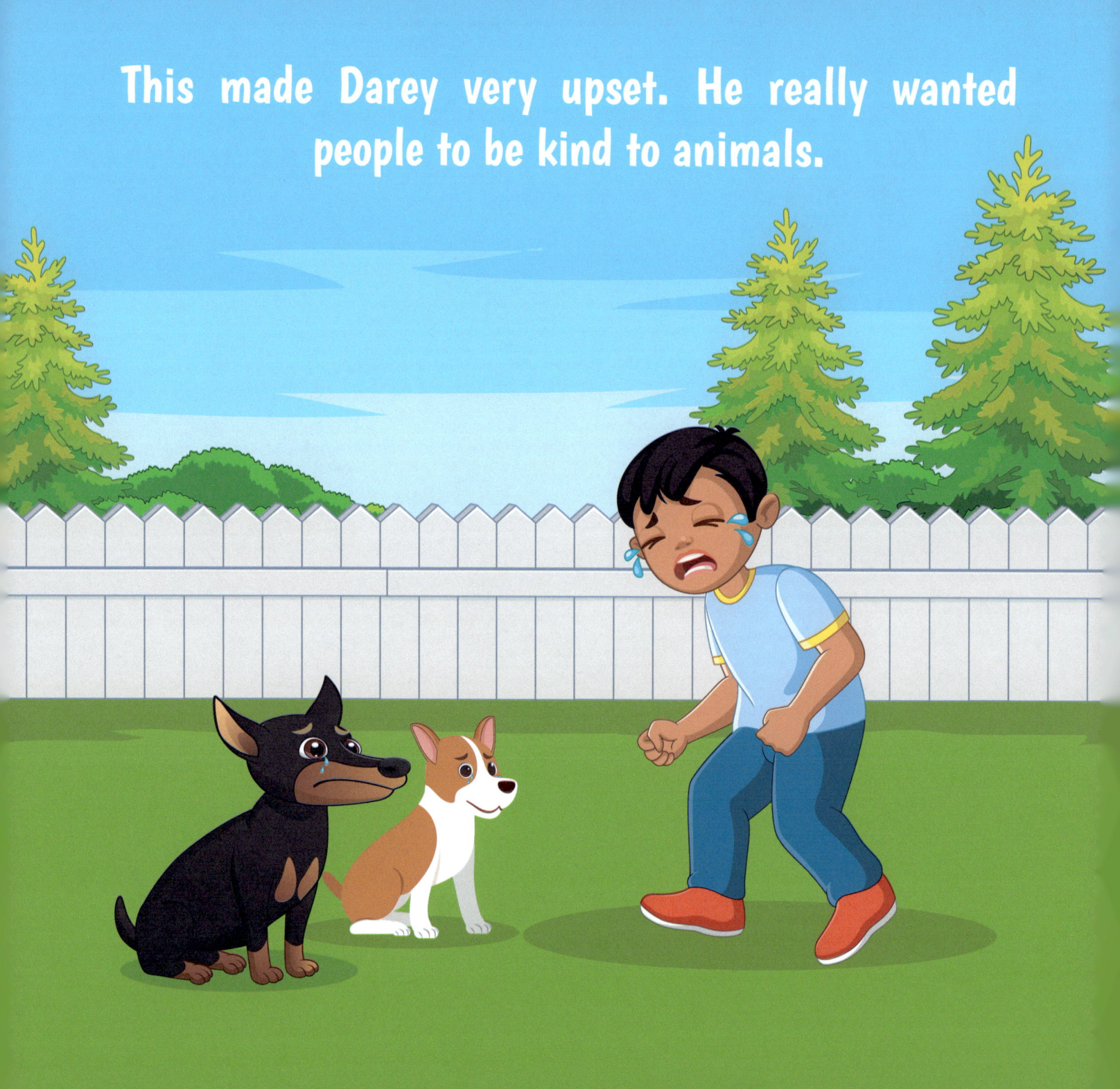
This made Darey very upset. He really wanted people to be kind to animals.

As Darey grew up, He asked God to show him how to teach kids to take care of their pets.

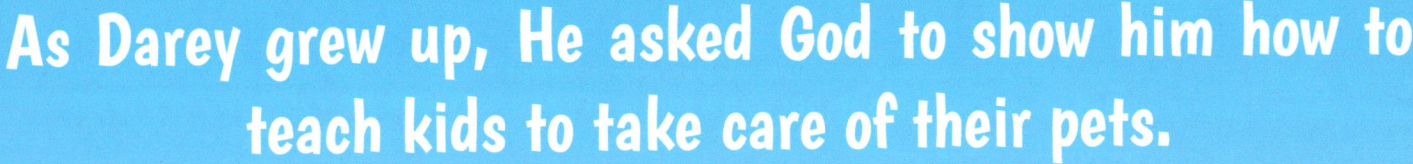

God answered his prayer. Darey started going to schools and churches with a mission organization called Ambassadors to the Nations, talking to children about ways to take care of their pets. Darey taught the children to. . .

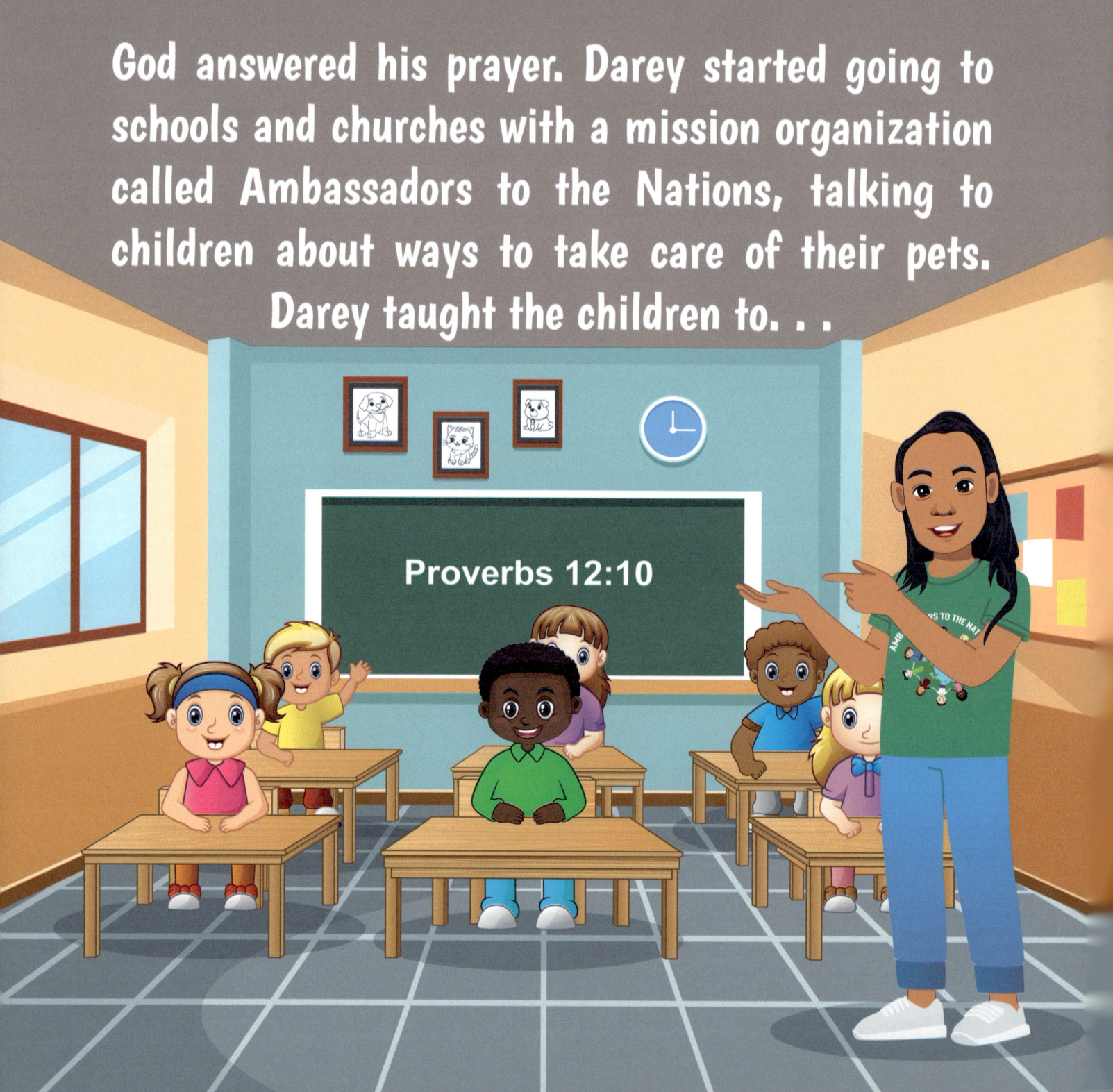

Make sure your animal has food and water every day.

Keep your pet clean. This is called grooming.

Make sure your animal has shelter when the weather is too hot, too cold, or rainy.

Never allow anyone to hurt or kick your pet!

Most of all, give your animals lots of love every day.

After Darey shared with the children about taking care of their animals, he gave each of them a coloring book to help them remember how to care for their pets.

Darey says, "Take care of animals. Your pet can be your best friend!"

HOW TO TAKE CARE OF YOUR ANIMALS/PETS

1. Feed and water your animals/pets every day.

2. Keep your animals/pets clean.

3. Make sure your animals/pets have shelter.

4. Never allow anyone to hurt your animals/pets.

5. Show your animals/pets how much you love them every day.

My Pet Pledge

I, _____ hereby pledge to:

1. Give my pet food and water every day.

2. Make sure my pet has shelter from heat, cold, and bad weather.

3. Keep my pet clean.

4. Never allow anyone to harm my pet, or other animals.

5. Pray for my pet.

6. Always show love to my pet. My pet is my BESTIE!

_____   _____

Signature   Date

Me and My Besties.

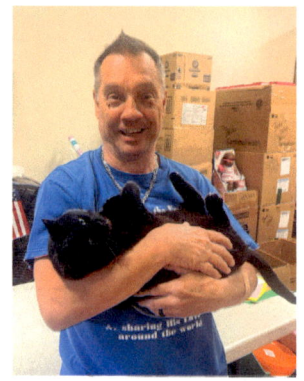

In 1990, on our first mission trip to Nigeria, Africa, the Lord spoke to Karen, "Would you be willing to have compassion on my people?" Karen responded, "Lord, I will." It was then that the Lord spoke to us to give our lives up for the nations. In 1992, the Lord called us to full-time missionary work and gave us Ambassadors To The Nations. Pastors Darey and Karen have been leading mission teams, building churches, schools, medical clinics, after-schools, feeding programs and more in Nicaragua, Mexico, Philippines, Cuba, Nigeria, Congo, Cameroon, India, Guatemala, Jamaica, Peru, and many other countries. We take to heart Psalm 2:8 and do our best to see this verse come to pass in the lives of the people wherever we minister.

"Ask of me, and I will give thee the nations for thine inheritance, And the uttermost parts of the earth for thy possession." - Psalm 2:8 (ASV) We hope this book will inspire children to love and care for their pets.

We want to say a special thanks to Bonita Lillie for all of her love and help in writing our children's books. (bonitalillie.com)

Our other children's books are Princess Ava Jo: A True Story and The Great Adventures of Poncho the Clown.

For more information about our missions, please go to ambassadorstothenations.com or Ambassadorstothenations@gmail.com

Made in the USA
Columbia, SC
10 May 2024